ROPES
In Four Rounds

ROPES: In Four Rounds
10th Anniversary Edition

Editor: Randall Horton
Author photo: Derrick Harriell

ISBN 979-8-9881655-6-9

Willow Books, a Division of Aquarius Press
www.WillowLit.net

Printed in the United States of America

Rounds

Four

Three

Two

One

To me, boxing is like a ballet—except there's no music,
no choreography,
and the dancers hit each other.
—Jack Handy

If they cut my bald head open, they will find one big boxing glove.
That's all I am. I live it.
—Marvin Hagler

Every time I hear the name Joe Louis my nose starts to bleed
—Tommy Farr

I made a lot of mistakes out of the ring, but I never made any in it
—Jack Johnson

for Brady X McKinley

Introduction

Our Ropes. This re-release.

Sometime in 2014, Beth Ann Fennelly, phenomenal writer and then Director of Creative Writing at University of Mississippi, messaged me and said that the program decided to offer me a Grisham Writers in Residence fellowship for the year 2015-2016. I'd never actually stayed a night in Oxford, as it was always talked about in my home of Jackson, Mississippi as the one place in the state you never ever wanted to visit, given its history of violent antiblackness and neoconfederacy.

Immediately, I looked at the faculty website and focused initially on one name, Derrick Harriell. We were black. We were bald. I assumed we had much of the same experiences of fighting off the ropes in academia and American literature. I'd read *Ropes* and frankly assumed that the black man who created the most textured, booming book on the literal and metaphorical art of boxing and four of the greatest boxers ever, couldn't find home in Oxford, Mississippi. I assumed. This rerelease. Let me slow it down.

I read *Ropes* on a train ride across the country. New York to Oakland. And the way Harriell moved in and out of persona, in and out of place, and smack dab into the experience of getting knocked out and needing to knock another human out for mobility, was something I hadn't read or felt in my readerly lifetime. No one does to a black boy's imagination what a brilliant boxer does. We often associate it with ability to punch, but it's also tied to the ability to take a punch. I knew that, but I did not actually know why. *Ropes* answered and asked better questions than I was capable of.

Ropes is the rare book that slips into, and then makes art of, the fleshy cracks in the hearts of the fighters and duckers in us. We are left, never alone, to piece together the jagged pieces that connect each of us to the most dominating fighters of our time. Harriell and I spent 5 years together in Oxford as colleagues. And boys. We talked boxing, getting hit, singular art, literary legacy and how to literally use the ropes in this life to our benefit. We loved each other whole, through art and laughter.

No one in the history of literature has written so profoundly about the ropes in our pugilistic giants' lives, and the ropes we must blur, disentangle and work to survive winning. And that is what Harriell has done for us. He has used gargantuan skill and will to chronicle the consequences of surviving winning and losing on the ropes as heartachy artists. The world was not ready to heed Harriell's plea to accept living on, under, off *Ropes*. We are here now. And *Ropes* is, as it was, waiting for us to enter, knowing we will never be the same when the book closes and our fights proceed. This rerelease. Our *Ropes*.

—Kiese Laymon, June 2023

The Blue Derrick: Harriell Writes Johnson, Louis, Frazier, and Tyson

Milwaukee, WI 1996

Kings,
I cut holes
through mama's
brand new towels—
unsullied white-slip
on secondhand black
swim trunks, stuff
an ice cube in my face,
tell the bully
let's get this shit on.

Sometimes I close blinds,
turn lights off, turn hurt
on, swing at dark until
fists-bombs bomb
dresser, plaster wall, until
closet door buckles
like knees, until
the jamb latch gets bodied,
the cradled rib bodied,
the imagined jawbone
unprettied. Cheeks bruised in this
here room, blacker
than blue, blacker than
Jack during rounds of solitude.

My parents never question
who's winning
these scraps, never question
who's calling me nigger, never question
the need in me, how history
repeats—and demons release
even before the bell rings.
They only remind me
that a Derrick is a crane

used to lift heavy,
that there's steel inside me,
and inside that steel
is a god-like operator
who never forgets
which buttons to hit.

Sometimes the world turns
dead and I find that towel
and swing and swing and swing
all over. Kings, my pops
used to drop game faded
sometimes, spitting hauntings
again and again. My early days
like them early rounds,
head open, pop's voice
cutting through my dread
from the corner, he's saying,
don't worry about size, D,
you'll never grow bigger than
Uncle Ray, but will go the distance,
long as you keep your eyes locked
on honor roll, your mind
your golden glove, your golden
ticket, and when that isn't enough
detonate them fist into a train and haul
them shadows back to the shadow
bellies that birthed them.

Chicago, IL
Winter 2003

Kings,
The freight elevator was down
which meant moving a couch
mammoth enough to throne
all four of you up five flights.
It took three brothers
to push and pull, to wrestle
and fight that damn thing

13

round tight corners, our feet
slipping like Quarry's
when Frazier caught him slipping
in round seven.
Not even the devil
would let him out the gates
for round eight.

The devastation of not being
allowed to die. The frustration
of the visible man
whose free
                 will is compromised.
Those mornings
you find yourself
radiant on the roof of some
high-rise and some scaredy-cat
pulls you from the ledge
of your birthright
believing he's a hero.

A week after moving to Chicago
a Nissan smacked the back
of my Olds. The *damn snow
made me do it*. The Southside
black ice and wind waved
a bitter welcome flag.

Three days before that
my bank account went sick,
sicker than granny, sicker
than Joppy's neck after
Hopkins played speedbag
with his head. Unanimous
decision like my decision
to cry two days ago. I cried
for never climbing into that ring.
I could've been
middleweight champ, not undefeated
but famous enough to talk my shit
to a bigoted journalist.

Kings, the night my brothers left
I shadowboxed alone
in my Hyde Park apartment,
moved methodically among
unpacked boxes at my feet,
all labeled "Chicago or bust,"
my straight right
tearing through anxiety
like Jack was waiting
on the other side of the door
to have a word with me,
like he didn't know
every movement I made exorcised
inherited wrecks, like the ones
when you're alone for the first time
all winter and those fists begin swinging
back at you, you don't know your chin
a depressed mirror until
it shatters, and nobody's counting
to ten, you'll never know how long
you've been sleep.

Detroit, MI
Fall 2013

Kings,
I'm standing outside the St. Regis
having a smoke imagining Marvin
doing something like this
right here. The Prince of
Soul smoking angel tears
to show the record is done. You see,
I did something for you,
made something only I could.
Let's call it a record of
bound songs bricklaying
my broken through your biographies.

But maybe I didn't get it all
right. Maybe, Mike, instead
of calling Ms. Givens a witch,
you would've asked Allah
what to do with heart-
sickness. Maybe
Frazier, if we all looked
deeper we'd know
you'd forgiven Ali
years ago. You'll trade
that mockery for a statue
in South Philly, the city
kneeling toward your glory
like clasped hands
toward sun.

And I don't know
if I've done right by you
Brown Bomber. I imagined
you'd call your father a *madman*,
crazy person, who, *makes love*
to the walls of some asylum.
But maybe you might've
called him *a sufferer*
of white terror, a hostage
of hell colliding with hopelessness,
maybe you would've told Jack
I miss him, maybe
Jack would've said
me too.

My one-year-old sees
a cardiologist and I call him
a fighter. I call them angels
whenever he stops breathing
because I know there's more
bouts, more decisions,
more technicalities, tear-
blurred visions for us.
Tell him Ali died in Manilla,
in round fourteen,

tell him resurrection
purely a style,
like southpaw, like brawler,
like peek-a-boo.

Oxford, MS
Spring 2023

Kings,
Her and I have this tendency
of punching threats
when nobody's watching,
we swing divorce haymakers
Wilder than Bronze Bomber
knockout blows. She says
I would've been an awful boxer, says
my hands could never
keep up with my gluttony,
screams I'm a virtuous
spouse underdog,
jabs how childish I am
when shadowboxing still.
Let it go, she says, *this is your life,*
you're a father and a mediocre writer. Kings,
let's throw a punching bag
parade, perform a canvas
serenade, swing a jump rope
jitterbug. We know we only
number one when someone kisses
the mat. Kings, stare down
all them losers slouched
over kitchen tables, eating
food the color of their faces, lying
to their children about all them wins
that never happened.

Round
Four

Cus D'Amato on Fear

I feed the fire and it becomes a roaring blaze
—Cus D'Amato

Catskill, NY 1980

He tells me he's afraid.
I tell him of the hero
and coward,
how *both feel the same*,
how fear's *a fire* and *friend*.

When *the deer crossing an open field*
spots the speeding Blazer
intent on blazing it to oblivion,
nature begins the survival process
causing the heart to beat faster,
the deer to get out of range.

But Mike is no deer
and these bums no Chevys.
When they find themselves deep
down dark alleyways and the reaper
a dance floor away,
they find themselves a wick
lit on each end, chained to
the beat of a *roaring blaze.*

Letters to Joe Frazier from Mike Tyson

Brooklyn, NY 1970

Joe,
I returned from the hospital,
and sat front row
as daddy spun mama
about the house
till she became a broken ballerina
in a blood-smeared tutu.

If my fists were bigger
than golf balls
I would've driven them
through his head
with an assassins'
intent, believing one bullet
could change the world.

Brownsville, NY 1977

Joe,
I'm the pigeon king,
a wizard with no wands,
a boy afraid of his own footsteps.

The air in the projects
is poisonous. There are
monsters who find what you love
break it slowly
like the neck
of my favorite bird.

This day I learned
that fear and fire
are lovers
intertwined so closely
they become one figure.

Catskill, NY 1980

Joe,
I've met God.
He's old and weak
white and bald.
We call him Cus
but I'm sure
only God could make
blood sport poetry.

We watch black and white
reels of great fighters
till I'm dizzy.
Till I'm vomiting
the speed of Louis,
the anticipation of Marciano.

Boxing is a symphony
of wills, an orchestra of skills.
I've studied your left hook
under careful eye,
played peek-a-boo
with the night,
buried my chin
into my sternum
shot son-of-a-bitch
from these thighs.

Not Joe Frazier: Tyson Writes Apology Letter

July 25, 1986

Joe,
Tomorrow I'll beat your boy like he stole
my favorite bird, like he robbed
Cus of air, like his last name
not Frazier. I respectively intend to crush
his ribs and will in one blow, smack
that kid round the ring, remind him
his name not Joe.

You'd do the same,
so cast no voodoo once this is done.
And although I've hung your posters
along the hallways of my ambition,
don't find yourself vengeful.

Or you too can feel the supernova,
what I'm told is a carnival in the head,
dancing elephants, singing monkeys
and floating beds. A boogeyman's bad hands,
a sinner's lullaby lyrics, the junkie's vision
when angels come to visit.

The Champ Wipes Down His BMW

crouches near the hood
she starts swingin
with the boys in tune
windows boom
black leather sweat suit, Adidas
blood-glove red. Mike,
sweeps towel across
headlights, remembers
Brittany, seductive jabs
on hotel doors.

As he circles the rig
Steven Tyler instructs
walk this way
talk this way.
And Mike tries,
but his mouth won't
allow it. Neither will
his legs, still scarred
with Brittany's burns.

At that moment he realizes
he should thank her.
The burn cooked Berbick.
The agonizing leak
on fight night
turned Mike a freak.
Just gimmie a kiss
ooh, a-like this.

Letters on Love: Mike Tyson Writes Muhammad Ali

I like to watch her like a tiger…
What I want is the extreme…
I want to ravish them
—Mike Tyson

I

Muhammad,
If men are measured in earnings,
then pharaohs must be measured in harems.
I approach the ring of romance
relentlessly, shoot Eros-esq
uppercuts of desire at long
legs and short lived repudiations.
I own them.

What's the worth of waist
belts without women
to decorate them?
Mansions without furniture.
I'm not into flutes Muhammad,
I make love like I make sport,
deliberate and devastating,
a tornado moved on, leaving
the ravaged to revel in their ruins.

II

Muhammad,
This bitch has lost her mind,
picked the wrong place, wrong time
to tell me she's unsatisfied,
that I'm unruly, aggressive,
unfaithful, manic, misogynistic, juvenile.

Barbara Walters refereed the ambush,
her little pointy nose a sword in my back.
She never sent us to neutral corners,
never gave a standing eight count

or asked if I could continue.
Robin stood taller than Mitch Blood Green,
her hot barrage of heavy blows
enough to melt iron.

III

Muhammad,
There is only one love in this life.
Like Muhammad
you spread your gospel
in rings worldwide, left verses
on the foreheads of foes.

Allah found me in a prison cell,
wiped me clean.
Now I know how it feels to willingly hit
your knees, open your hands,
let something in.

Lady Lazarus: Robin Givens Speaks

Dying
Is an art, like anything else.
I do it exceptionally well.
—"Lady Lazarus" Sylvia Plath

I come from a line of long-legged
women with iron chins.
Sometimes when you fall
in love, hardwood floors
are your only catching-net.
Grandma could walk a tightrope
balance back-to-the-head blows.
Sometimes you're love struck
by an unabashed fist. Sometimes
Diablo wears lipstick, pumps
six-inch pitchfork tips.

I don't know the real reaper,
who harvested darkness.
I know making love was like
almost dying, the feathery fingertips,
the flashbacks. I often found
myself gracing a dark tunnel
a model's concentration,
the bright light hypnotic,
my crimson songs kryptonite.

Buster Douglas Provides Blow by Blow Instructional on Overcoming the Bully

I thank God. The only man I fear is God—Buster Douglas

Tokyo Dome, Tokyo
February 11, 1990

When yo mamma dies
right before a fight
a man grows Herculean pride.
Most times, the bully
beats you with his eyes,
packs lava behind his retina
and soon you believe you fighting
a giant. They was lying
when they said Bunyan was eight feet tall,
his ox elephant sized.
He was merely a man who believed
one chop at a time.

Tonight, an Angel named Lula Pearl
will glide me to the ring
and sing gospels that cloak me invincible.
World, I can't feel me feet anymore,
that devilish mug don't scare me anymore.
I'll park my right hook on his left eye
till it's no longer open for business,
swing my ax steady, steady till I hear
the crunch of a trunk on its last bone.
Oh hallelujah, I am Job.
There's a treasure chest in Tyson's jaw,
a box of blessings in these fists.

Michael Gerard Tyson's Rap Sheet

1978—Tyson at twelve is arrested
for confusing some senior citizen's purse
with his own.

June 21, 1987—The tongue is a machete:
an attempted kiss becomes
assault with a deadly.

Aug 23, 1988—When Mitch Green screams to Harlem
Tyson's pretty bird is conjuring pretty breakfast
in a green kitchen, the crowd hopes he can run fast.
Once smoke becomes ash, a broken bone and dilapidated eye
rests on the Harlem concrete, a check
Blood Green couldn't cash.

Sept 4, 1988—The engine in his BMW boils
like the one in his head. Sometimes suicide
annihilates the tree instead.

Oct 2, 1988—A robin's song on repeat
can drive a man to kill a living room,
to clothesline the chair, leg lock the table,
run a tornado through the tiny nest.

Dec 15, 1988—The left hand don't know
what the right hand do. Isn't it true
our hands possess free will.
If they find themselves moving
cross some stranger's backside,
should the whole
be held accountable?

April 26, 1989—When life becomes a drag
it is best to race it.

Aug 17, 1990—Enough sexual harassment suits to fill
a small library. The shelves won't tell the story,
the card catalogue will never collect dust.

March 26, 1992—This is the big one, the rope,
the firing squad. Landmines in stilettos
are undefeated. They swing perfume laced
body blows, expire you
with Aphrodite's girdle.

A Prison Lullaby

Indiana Youth Center, April 1992

Hush little pugilist embrace your digs.
Rest your soul in the pit of my rib.
Allow this harmony of monstrous moans
to melt you into the gut of my cold.
Bang these bars like Catskill bags.
Ferocious solitude cape you bad.
See little pugilist it's not so grim.
You're just one stint from martyrdom.

Jamaal X Jackson converts Mike to Islam

Indiana Youth Center, 1993

See, there's puppets, masters, and puppet masters
and minions, and minions to the minions
and bad ass wolves in Stacey Adams
who tap dance on roots, and by roots
I don't mean the nappy curb on your forehead
but that river running through your dream.
You see it before laying your dome
on a steel bench, it wakes you
screaming, looking to punch anything
with two eyes. Brother don't you know
Jesus was from Bed-Stuy, that Mary
was a jazz singer from Harlem. Don't you know
you come from sophisticated songbirds,
that there's a Viduidae in your tree.
You're more than a bad nigger
with a bad knee, more than your fornications,
than the knives flying out your eyes.
Rejoice in knowing we're all an X
away from sunshine.

The Lion Whisperer: Monica Turner Believes

I love these big cats as a mother loves her children…
They can be subdued but never conquered,
except by love
—Mabel Stark

Our courtship witnessed by cold
metal bars took snapshots
while mustached guards with guns
provided the grimy backdrop
and soon my words were petting
the untamed feline numb, rule one,
you must never show fear.

I said I wanted to be his doctor,
he wanted to be my donor.
I whispered about the stethoscope,
its ability to locate absent hearts,
the scalpel beneath my tongue.
I promised a revival,
a baptizing of some sort, a surgery,
a procedure to jumpstart the soul.
I vowed to be more than a friend or mother.
I was made to be his keeper,
to do what Mabel Stark had once done,
lay a warm hand on a wild thing,
to each morning count both
my blessings and fingers.

Tupac Shakur Reads Letter from Mike Tyson

Ain't no way in hell, that I could ever be a rapist
—Tupac Shakur

Clinton Correctional Facility, New York 1995

Pac,
I've been where you are,
rubbed palm against
concrete walls, confusing the cold
rigid surface for a woman,
no, a cadaver. I know what
it is to be accountable, to make
love with a crown on your head,
for jesters to juggle
during the romantic hour.

Prison is no place for gods,
it'll yank stars out you, and once
they've taken your stars
they'll come for your moons.

I wish I was warned of how
roses can be keys to prison doors,
how the word *rapper* can be mistaken
for *rapist*, how sodomy and slavery
sometimes look the same in the dark.

They'll try to make a dragon
out of you, show your fire
on the six o'clock news,
try to make you forget your mother's
songs. But, when the cellblock's
silent the rhythm will return, the 808s
burning in your throat
like Hennessey, your voice
enough to make speakers bleed.

Undressing the Belt

Las Vegas, NV
March 16, 1996

Just yesterday I was with him,
the humble Brit who loved

watching me at a distance,
a gentleman

often out of breath
from hours of rope jumping

afraid of my marching shoes.
We both knew

I was unsatisfied,
that it took a real bull

to keep me
in one place, a willing warrior

to loosen leather straps,
remove the locked buckle

locate the key
that undresses me.

Canine to Cartilage

Las Vegas, NV
June 28, 1997

I'm tired of talking.
You don't seem to understand l'art pour l'art,
you don't understand beauty.
Your problem is your esteem
your stifling deformity.

Must be a burden to resemble a cloven hoof
or dismantled shiitake.
I get to be a pyramid inverted
responsible for both love and death marks,
have slipped more ropes than Black Herman
more bras than Clark Gable.

Tonight I'll weigh down on your belly
like an unforgiving guillotine
until onlookers become puzzled
by the bloody puzzle in the ring.

Animal Planet

....some of these birds are world champions
—Mike Tyson

re-airs an episode of *Taking on
Tyson*, the one where Iron Mike
leans on a tenement ledge
and beckons his team of birds
who wing through matter as if
last one home a rotten egg, or
some sexy pigeon lover awaits within
that rooftop coop.

*Pigeons have had their place
during some memorable moments
in history*, Mike avows
as if he means this very one,
that tomorrow's records will tell
the tale of the tape,
down to the hollering
face tattoo.

A year ago
HBO re-aired *The Hangover*
and Iron Mike revealed
his very best
Phil Collins karaoke, heavy balled fist
air drums and all. Real
soul snatching vocals
and atom splitting air drums.

And all the players were so afraid
of Tyson playing Tyson
they drove down the Strip
with a drugged-up tiger
sleep in back,
not once asking
what the animal's dreams

might sweet like.
What it's nightmares
might sting like.

Round
Three

Billy Boy Frazier Floats
A Message Down the Beaufort River

Beaufort, SC 1956

Dear Jack,
Poppa donate a arm to a moonlit field,
say sometimes when you pumped with moonshine
your heart a hay-filled wagon you just drag around.
When I was born,
the witch-lady say I got to think like a left arm
so poppa can dig up his smile.
Now, he don't feel like he lost no arm
and when Ugly Man Mitch come spitting in poppa face,
a shovel to the head was a left hook he never saw.

Letters to Joe Louis from Joe Frazier

Philadelphia, PA 1962

Joe,
Philly colder than Rosetta's stare
after she found I'd been laying with Flo.
Told her it don't matter cause all the babies need heat,
so I send hot bills back to Beaufort
and once in a while a few pounds of meat.

Been boxing too,
Philly fools got two left feet,
wonder how I hit hard with no practice,
I tells them luck, but truth is
when the slaughterhouse turn quiet and manager gone,
I'm surrounded by armies of departed livestock.
I introduce my fists to hanging ribs
and feel spirits moving bout me,
dance like it's midnight,
swing hard when blood reach my eye.

Tokyo, Japan 1964

Joe,
Buster beat me but beat himself in turn.
They calling my left hook a train,
say it make a man meet his maker,
hump the canvas like a wet dream.

*New York, NY
February 16, 1970*

Joe,
At Madison Square,
in a sixteen by sixteen square,
Ellis face found the square grill

of a round glove,
pitched a tent on the mat,
cried uncle from a wooden stool.

Conspiracy Theory: or Divine Intervention?

Lewiston, ME
May 25, 1965

Tonight you'll swear the Yeti sleeps open-eyed,
scream business of Malcolm and Muslims
Muhammad and mix ups. You'll blame
the FBI, CIA, Bumpy this or Pretty Boy that
call a tall blonde stewardess to see
what she knows. She'll tell you
bout Jews and horse tracks,
pedigrees and debts, dope and casinos.
Later you'll drink pints,
lay it out for the gray hair
behind the bar. He'll listen
till you're gone then tell your ghost
all bout you, bout you being in deep,
call the pigs, propose an elaborate stakeout,
help'em tap the digs.

Aficionados loop the punch
in their heads for years to come,
slow it down when they think they see
shadows, freeze the frame at two minutes
twelve seconds, remember that Jesus
had twelve disciples, two lives
and that seven goes into fourteen exactly
two times.

Ali's Empty Cell Calls Him Out

I'm so fast that last night I turned off the light switch
in my hotel room and was in bed before the room was dark.
—Muhammad Ali

Clay can't keep from shaking at his shadow
so scared he changing inside and out,
done changed his name he so scared.
Sometimes some things so pretty
they start to look ugly, just real ugly.
The problem with ugly folks is they don't know
when they ugly, try and distract you by running
their mouth. Clay real good at running.
Somebody told him bout my record,
fifteen, one eighty sevens served death
sentences to make a sage chain smoke.
Stop running Clay, come get it over with.
We can write poems if you'd like
bout butterflies and bees, rhyming sonnets or haikus
while I kung fu you for a few.

Recapping Ali vs. Frazier I:
As Told by Ringside Journalist

Madison Square Garden, NY
March 8, 1971

Ladies and gentlemen,
it was billed as *The Fight*,
the holy war, Allah versus Christ,
butterfly lips colliding with fists.
It didn't disappoint.
As Hollywood selected sides,
Ali turned the ring ice,
orbiting Frazier like an angry satellite,
crimson fists fast
like meteorites.

Joe battled.
A determined lumberjack
stalking a tree,
a pissed off bull seeing blood,
a big bad wolf blowing feverishly.
Ali's kidney's
asked to see an imam
in round fifteen, drank coffee
with Frazier's broken jaw
in a hospital cafeteria
the following morning.

Recapping Ali Frazier I:
As Told by Frank Lucas

Teaneck, New Jersey
March 9, 1971

So I found myself pimping, moving prettier
than Ali down the red carpet,
the dame on my arm
turning more heads than Hepburn
in *My Fair Lady*, a chinchilla
wrapping me hotter than a hot Christmas
gift sparkling beneath a glowing tree.

All of Hollywood showed
to hear one pretty note
from my mouth, one rhyme of wisdom
to change a cat's religion.

It was never bout Ali or Frazier,
this was a clash of gold, fur and heroin,
of no jive hocus pocus
capable of death blows.
I don't know who won the damn fight,
I know my heroine delivered me
to the Gestapo, who took photos
and salivated at the image
of my wealthy body dangling
from a red, white and blue tree.

Joe Frazier and The Knockouts

Donegal, Ireland
June 8, 1971

do-re-mi backstage, rehearse
the pain on his face tells me
my left hook had caught him,
ruffled tuxedo shirt red
says he's serious, black
satin lapel sparkles, patent
leather feet eager
to slide like Ruffin.
Joe is feinting backstage
twirling, his wrists thick
with gold, voice grit
cinnamon. The mirror reflects
spins, Brown-like
stunts, bells and whistles
to faint a flower-child.

Marvis Frazier Bears Witness

When my father fell the first time, I started laughing
—Marvis Frazier

Kingston, Jamaica
January 22, 1973

Daddy a man, unstoppable.
He not afraid of no George,
not afraid of no fight.

I never seen so many black
black people ever,
this must be Africa's brother.

George come out dropping haymakers
and daddy so funny how he toying,
doing that dance that make people dizzy.

If little Africa this black, how black
is big Africa. Probably black as daddy's
fists when pulled out ice.

I hope we get this over quickly
and head back to Philly.
But George keep swinging

like we wronged him,
like I took his son's lunch money,
like he don't know

daddy don't lose.

Ali Frazier II: Ali's Gloves Deliver Punch line

Madison Square Garden, NY
January 28, 1974

Two boxers walk into a ring.
But Joe forgot the one about the angry nigger
with the flat nose, the one that takes twelve rounds
and a lot of blood to hash out.

Two boxers walk into a ring.
One, a dancing Adonis,
the other, an awkward Neanderthal.
An appetizer of hate
feeds the Garden before the bell
foreshadows the pending ass whooping.

Two boxers walk into a ring.
Sportsmanship had been discarded
several black eyes ago,
decency hid its head in a dark hole.
Frazier had been tired of our shit
and game planned a funeral for Ali's mouth.

Two boxers walk into a ring.
But Joe forgot the one about the angry nigger
with the flat nose, the one that takes twelve rounds
and a lot of blood to hash out.

Mistress in Manila:
Veronica Porche Testifies

Manila, Philippines
September, 1975

Manila is an endless Sam Cooke number
where Muhammad is the record
and I the needle.
Our tune posed
like mannequins in storefront windows,
burning spectacle
like a cross in Georgia,
Alabama, or Mississippi.

We honeymooned
before crossing the broom, I in yellow,
prettier than a virgin canary,
a halo atop Ali's afro,
a sin pinned against his dimples,
a strongbox for abandoned poems.

He never believed Frazier was a gorilla.
Nor was the Uncle Tom remark
made sincerely.
It all was a speed bag for a lethargic marriage.
A knock knock crack
with a straight right punch line.

Belinda hated his jokes as well,
and after networks fed our presidential visit
to TV's back home,
she grew wings and flew here.
Focused as a fighter pilot,
more formidable than Frazier.

Mug Reupholster

Araneta Coliseum, Philippines
October 1, 1975

At their best these hands
can repair a cloud
torn by lightening, an eye
severed by leather.
When my fighter drops
to his stool, suicide notes
in his face, I fix him.
Dear audience,
observe the Elephant Man
become John Wayne,
a soul so close to moaning
the white flag sends
another cut man into
his bag of miracles.

Shot For Joe:
One Part Marciano / Two Parts Frazier

Nothing a little bullshit can't fix,
a few laps round Philly
being pursued by poor kids
who'd never believe a five-two
heavyweight champ is cool.

Nothing a little make believe can't knock out,
southpaw Fairy Dust mixed with
left hook bullshit. Peter
pan the camera round me
as I circle raw meat
that don't swing back
just like Joe said he did.

Be sure my face is showered red with dye,
show me how to be bad.
Film me chasing chickens
and rubber balls, dress me
in soulful fedora, some black
leather gloves, catch me
snapping fingers next to doo-wopping
street brothers on Philly street corners.

Leave no room for questions,
let poetry fall from my awkward jowl.
Write in a woman for me to love,
someone who believes I can beat
Apollo Creed, that Clubber Lang
won't make her a widow.

Frazier's Black and Blue Dream

Chain me
at the ankles,
paralyze the foot taps
inside me.
Ali a colorful dashiki
draping my shoulders,
a monkey I wear
as I wander a field
of cracked fists.

Heaven a ring
of clouded ropes,
Little Walter's harmonica
moaning like a ex-wife
in a Chicago summer cot.

I'm melting silhouette
gagged by B.B.'s strings,
and shadowy fingers pluck
at my face till blue
notes drop from my mouth
from my chin into
gutbucket tunes that roll me
out of bed and send me
sparring with still
black little me's.

Dear Darkness: Joe Frazier writes Mike Tyson

the beauty of the dream vanished, and breathless horror
and disgust filled my heart
—Victor Frankenstein (in Mary Shelley's *Frankenstein*)

Philadelphia, PA 1981

There was no laboratory,
only bones and worn eye sockets
we give the gods
of bloody gloves.

Your destiny is no mystery
no puzzle or secrets why you here.
You must destroy everything.

They won't understand you Mike.
The crosses you throw at old women,
shitty bird cages you lay round.

They will understand your wreckage,
the overcast inside, the howling thunder
that sends Prometheus running.

Old Joe's Museum of Antiques

Is it home? Wherever you want to make your home
—Joe Frazier

Philadelphia, PA 2005

Leather belts caked with
dust grow old in corners
and curl into cobwebbed hammocks.
Boxes enclosing rusted trophies,
medals, old magazine cutouts
surround Joe's bed.

A nylon duffel bag that once encased
29-0 gloves now hold damaged
film of Ali versus Frazier, all three.
And if you want,
old Joe will wear his docent cap
and walk you through each fight,
each round, each punch,
scream and swing, making sure
you feel as if you're really there.

Round
Two

Letters to Jack Johnson from Joe Louis

Rural Alabama, 1925

Jack,
They say my father a madman, crazy person
makes love to the walls of some asylum,
I don't know him.

I know new father likes to drive.
Last night zoomed into a pool of piranhas
wearing white hoods and punchy looks.
Mother shivered like someone told her
they've seen father's ghost
near Buckalew Mountain, new father
held fear across his face.

I recalled the fire-ball game
my sister and I use to play,
how we'd kerosene a ball of rags,
set them aflame.
As the glowing rags
flew back and forth,
I often wondered if my hands
were incapable of feeling heat,
or perhaps the flames were my fists.

Detroit, MI 1930

Jack,
My mother wants me to become
a musician, the Catherine Street Gang
their muscle. My fingers have problems
locating the strings of a violin
but none in curling themselves inward
to form a wishing well.
I'm developing a reputation
for right and left handed
knockout gas, a violin case
with a canon inside.

Detroit, MI 1932

Jack,
Nowadays Detroit is birthing fighters
like Tin Lizzie's. Seduced me.
Promised Jim Crow
don't go in the ring,
that the language of
the fourteenth amendment lies
within those ropes.

There are no exhibitions.
You beat up the man
in front of you before he drags you
to the cotton field
you came from.

Last summer I floored Otis,
used his falling figure to collapse
a domino of thirteen men.
We couldn't be more
polar Jack, no one fears
the golden shadow I cast.
On a snowy afternoon
I could pass   for them,
for a college kid,
a boy about to play Brahms.

Good For Nothing Joe

Folks I know can't understand
Why I must have that man
Lord, he sends me like nobody can
—Lena Horne "Good For Nothin' Joe"

Pompton Lakes, NJ
June, 1935

She was young, her mouth
fainted men my trainer's years,
men who'd been round the world
making it with women twice her soul.
But you wouldn't know
when she's sitting across from you
firing the dirtiest nothings
out the cleanest chops.
I told her to clean her language,
she told me to fuck off.
We both knew all I wanted was to fuck on,
build an alter in her hair,
blow blues on her horn.

The Radio Sounds Better Than Cab Calloway When Crooning a Louis Fight

Chicago, IL
June 22, 1937

They want me to croon
a tune that turns the night yellow
giving all permission to lose
a tooth or lover,
want Louis to pull off
what Jack had, want him
to win it bad.
And so purple lips blow smoke
gray fists cut invisible
the way Braddock cut Joe
at the knees.

Braddock right to the chin
has sent Louis down
Joe Louis is down

Except Joe don't know the blues
scats a swing
Braddock never learned

And they tangle
Joe lands a right cross to the head
and a right cross to the head
and a right cross
to the head

a broken ditty with background
music howls the noise
a man makes when biceps
keep on beating
the belt off his waist.

The Brown Bomber Convinces Benny
He a Man

Chicago, IL
June 22, 1937

Joe Louis champ and I feel strange tonight,
hear trumpets outside my window,
taste a lean in my bourbon.
My old lady flashed a bosom at the final bell
whispered sugar in my ear,
told me I could stop a train.

A man does what he wants,
so I'm gone smoke till my head a chimney,
till Santa white ass burned black
as Jack Johnson's fingertips
resting on the fiery breasts
of some jacked-up coal burner.

Constructing The New Negro

If Joe lost we were back in slavery and beyond help...
-Maya Angelou

Yankee Stadium, NY
June 22, 1938

A white towel can remove
dirt from coal stained fingertips
or blood from a blotched forehead,
it can make things go away.
One year after that Brown Bomber
put a family of towels
to the body of James Braddock
a collection of nerves line the ring.

Word in the Bronx is blood
will parachute through Yankee Stadium
like a Babe Ruth fireball
or holy oil through a congregation.
But shortly after the bell
it becomes the white towel
next to the wailing German
that removes a tension in the breeze,
a grin from a Nazi face.

Lena's Note to her Estranged Joe

New York, NY
1940

My fingers say without you
they nothing, worthless flesh, bone
not been nowhere
grabbed nothing but whiskey and wrinkled
bags of smack. These ears
say no melody better
than your love confessions
the castles you create as we lay
listening to Ellington and Calloway.
There's a zoo of sad songs
inside my chest. I sing
to smashed audiences
looking to love me posthumously.

Ray Robinson Refuses to Fight Jimmy Doyle

The night before the fight with him, I dreamed in my sleep that
I'd knocked him out and he died in the ring
—Ray Robinson

Cleveland, OH June 24ᵗʰ, 1947

I'm no fortune-
teller, but know
I was shown
my left arm shimmering
all flickering like a fire-
arm, the way it shot from my hip
a whole bunch of evil.
It scrambled, all unforgiving, clawing
through the world impatiently
like "Colored" signs
that can't wait
to hurt.

Marciano Deconstructs The New Negro

Last Of Unusually Inspiring Star
Lethargic, Old, Unfit, Inept, Sad
—Detroit News Headline

Madison Square Garden, NY
October 26, 1951

In my dressing room I undress
tape casing thumping knuckles.
Journals and microphones bound me
to shadows in fedoras who want to know how
I outclassed the Negro.

They scream Louis was old,
out of shape, speculate
what this means
for meatballs and spaghetti
jazz, the Mason-Dixon line.

I think about how tough
it must have been for miei genitori,
how quickly a violent Atlantic
can change a history.
I wonder if Joe felt
like a drowning boat,
how his passage through ropes
shook a sob out Sugar Ray.

Uncle Sam Shows Joe Louis the Ropes

Half of it went to wine, women and song....
the other half I wasted
- Joe Louis

Fall, 1954

There's no way out Joe,

pay what you owe.
If Marciano beat you

through ropes with a glove,
imagine what I'll do

bare knuckled.
I've watched you duck and dodge

bob and weave
believe that agreeable

equals invisible,
I see everything.

You're more like Jack
than you know.

I wasn't stunned
when you accepted keys

to the pastry store, pointed
like a child to spoils

you couldn't afford.

Round
One

Joe Jeanette and Sam McVey Fistfight in Hell

...we climbed up, he first and I second,
so far that I saw through a round opening
some of the fair things that heaven bears
- Dante

April 17th 1909, Paris France

We tried wrecking each other's face
for forty-nine rounds, enough time
for a child to be pulled out a mother's womb
or a man to be lynched.
For three and a half hours,
the time it took mama to make
thanksgiving dinner, or revive daddy,
we beat each other's ass
like it came with forty acres, two mules
one hundred bibles.

I'm not sure what it is about Paris
that readies a man for his maker.
A few years back, Du Bois introduced this city
to the improved Negro.
Black faces furnished Paris sidewalks,
paintings and poems echoed new theories.

Du Bois didn't prophesize today's massacre,
there were no photos of the metamorphosis
our bodies would undergo.
I laid on the canvas so often I almost
fell in love with it. Sam and I traded so much blood
I almost fell in love with him.
If dying on two feet is possible
I'm sure I've done that.
I've granted wishes to women ringside,
dropped cherubs in the crowns of hats.

Letters to Jack Johnson from Robert Delaney

From Sea, October 1855

Jack,
I learned early on
my fists had always been free
to roam, you will learn this too.
As a child I collapsed
young Negro boys,
watched spirits buckle
like canned oysters.

Liverpool, UK 1862

Jack,
I am keeper of the beast.
Left those Baltimore roads
my vagrant father once stumbled down.
Manchester's a sight for Negro eyes.
Black sailors scatter crowded streets
in search of women
and sport. Just yesterday I saw
an English woman holding
a Negro's hand
as if it mattered.
Liverpool offered love
for me Jack. Here, I settled
a gambling debt
pushed a man's nose
into his face.

Point of Ayr, Wales
September 15, 1863

Jack,
Today I fought a giant whose snarls
have sent men to mothers
without a shot being thrown.
I did not invite fear
despite the circus in my knees.

Fifty pounds is enough
to change things. The gods
sent rain and hail.
Round three began with Harry swinging
hell, and for a moment I forgot
where the hell I was. Jack,
if Hell is anything like the ring,
do not be afraid.
There are no chains
inside, and Satan sometimes
has a glass chin.

Jack Johnson writes Robert Delaney

Galveston, Texas 1888

Robert,
This morning mamma told of a Negro,
arms iron cannonballs,
hammer heads for hands.
Said an honest man
would always best machines
and being strong
more godly
than tricking folks.
But I'm a strong and honest
trickster, like Henry
whose bout ended
with that hammer
in tears.

Mamma then lift my shirt,
told me firm up, poked
my chest, squeezed
my arms, and through
a bent grin said *Baby*
u gon' be stronger
than that man
I' been tellin' you bout.

Los Angeles, CA
February 3, 1903

Robert,
It took twenty rounds
a little blood
to get rid of Denver Ed.
That hardheaded Negro
kept punching, even after
I told him stay down.
I never cared much
bout no colored belt,

this America,
and even white boys
climb into frocks
one arm at a time.

Sydney, Australia
December 26, 1908

Robert,
Bust up Burns in fourteen rounds.
I've never seen no Negro lynched
but understand the mercy
their eyes beg for.
Damn mercy,
that mob in Springfield
hung that barber
showed no pity, paraded
his charred body for blocks,
wanted to show
they not fooling round.

Robert, should beating a man
in front of his wife and kids
feel this good?
I don't feel like just no fighter.
When they said I was champion
of all the world,
I didn't feel like just no champion.

Saturday Night at *Cafe de Champion*, as Told by Dizzy the Barkeeper

Chicago, IL August 1912

Round one Jack swaggers in
yielding the familiar shake,
the bouncing floor beneath
our soles, shaking with each
giant step, like heaven ripped
out falls Johnson, three piece
threads, cigar jabbed
in iron jaw, a king sketched
in smoke, glowing
like sweat laced gloves.
Rag muse fingered at piano keys.
All for this communion
all night long.

The champ sits
with white babe who not his
wife, but shines like Maude Adams.
The dick alone thinks
he's undercover.
The bellbottom offers
whores his government jack.
Round two,
Etta floats in fried,
over to Jack's table
and with eyes
sketches horns
out his shiny head.
The Maude looking broad
hauls a bourbon to
an empty stool,
Jack offers Etta
the hole she's left.

Etta Duryea's Suicide Note

I want to be buried in Chicago… let me rest for once
—Etta Duryea

Chicago, IL September 1912

O Jack,
I'm a litany of holes, been feeling mad, crazy
cuckoo bird on a collapsing wire
baby, on nights you're gone, I roll
reels in wallpaper, you boxing
beneath bedcovers. O I suppose
I've never been good at marriage. Clarence
made me a statuette, you made me
a crown and almost marched
to the doors of the White
House, you tried curing me, calming
constellations I found when clocked silly.
O darling I've prayed
in silence, in chaos, on knees, asked
the big questions, to the big Him, pleaded
that He keep you pinned, tightly
attached to His lapel.

Found—
Jack Johnson Goes to Jail:
Court Refuses Cash Bail and He Cannot find Bondsmen

The New York Times
November 9, 1912

Jack Johnson,
champion heavyweight pugilist of the world,
tonight occupied, a cell
in the County Jail
due to his failure to furnish
a $30,000 bond for his release
on the beastly charge of sleeping
with a white woman.

As he left the Federal Building,
handcuffed to Deputy Marshall Ed,
after a futile plea
not to have his wrists manacled,
Johnson seemed greatly dejected.
And in his extended fight
to reduce years,
he shed tears.

Doormen Left and Charlie
Banter Outside the Cotton Club

Harlem, NY 1924

Charlie you show said some truth.
       But, I did hear bout one night
Jack was pushed on by a few assholes.
I wasn't there, cousin Benny was.
Say Jack sat smoking a cigar,
them expensive kinds.
These boys surround him
with beer bottles and plantations
in they fists. Now Etta seemed scared,
but not Jack. He just smoked.
Then one land a sucker punch
to the soft side of Jack's jaw.
Etta screamed like she seen a haint,
the giant didn't split a nose hair.
       Tonight for yo' delight,
the queen of blues
will sooth yo' mood.
       Let me cut to the meat.
Benny say smoke came out Jack ears,
and his eyes look like burning buildings.
The government tried to hide this,
but I knows the truth. In summer of eleven,
on the south side of Chicago, there was a hurricane
weather folks couldn't explain.
Go to Lake Calumet and look in the water
real hard. You gone see pissed off people
staring up at you, shattered blocks and teeth
floating long-side the bottom.

There are Ghosts Inside Here:
Jack Johnson writes Joe Louis

United States Penitentiary, Leavenworth August 1920

Joe,
There are ghosts inside here,
floating men abandon their youth each hour.
Youngblood called me black Moses
before hanging himself with a rusted dream.
We take turns dying.

Lucille's become a haiku,
three lines neatly tucked in an envelope
and delivered to the doorstep of my imagination.
I've fallen in love with my hands,
realizing their potential for putting things together.
Some days, my fingers twist,
sweat streams my face and,
I'm in that ring again, satisfied.
Across is an executioner,
red fist,
trying to decapitate my smile.

Joe Jeanette Laments Not Getting Shot

Jack forgot about his old friends after he became champion
and drew the color line against his own people
—Joe Jeanette

I'm not one of them, yet
ghosts dig themselves into me, taunt
terrorize, seethe inside my black
skin, ask the difference
between Jack and I, dump
punches I can't duck.

I'm no stand-in, no
spar-bag, no
colored fist.
Sometimes a season
separates a champ
from treasure. Sometimes
the coward is a faux emperor
an unfired bullet to the back
a nude ruler whose bone smile
can charm even
a child.

Sam McVey Writes Galveston Giant Letter from Grave

Mount Olivet Cemetery, NY
December, 1921

Way I went way
down deep
thought I was sleep, well
awake but sleep
like when a banshee
get on top, make love
to you and you
can't move
a knuckle.

Least now they
can find me. Jack
I'm gone be
down deep
rooted low
a hum
in the mud
all muddy
with dignity.

Jack Johnson's Automobile Commits Suicide

Dr. W.D. Allison said that the 68 year-old Negro died
from internal injuries and shock- NY Times June 11ᵗʰ, 1946

Everything around you kills itself,
Etta, now me. You've placed the most beautiful women
in these seats. The thighs of actresses have laid
on this very leather. I am not afraid to go Jack,
there's a better me on the assembly line
as we speak. Except this one won't ride as softly,
it'll come screaming into this life,
smashing whatever's in the goddamn motherfucking way.

Tale of the Tape

Muhammad Al— professional record of 56 W/ 5 L 37 KO's is well known for his fight trilogy with Joe Frazier amongst his many notable bouts and iconic status.

Joe Louis Barrow—professional record of 66 W/ 3 L 52 KO's is well known for his bouts with German boxer Max Schmeling and the cultural and political spectacle surrounding these fights. Louis was the first black heavyweight champion since Jack Johnson. His romantic affair with famed singer Lena Horne is also well documented.

Robert Delaney—professional record unconfirmed later changed his name to Bob Smith and is one of the earliest documented US born black pugilists.

James "Buster" Douglas—professional record of 38 W/ 6 L 25 KO's is most known for his shocking upset of then champion Mike Tyson on 02/11/1990.

"Smokin" Joe Frazier—professional record of 32 W/ 4 L 27 KO's is well known for his fight trilogy with Muhammad Ali, as well as his open bitterness toward Ali who throughout promotional tours taunted Frazier with racially insensitive insults.

Marvis Frazier—professional record of 19 W/ 2 L 8 KO's is Joe Frazier's son.

Joe Jeanette—professional record of 83 W/ 10 L 70 KO's is one of the early black heavyweight boxers and is most known for his 49 round bout with Sam McVey: the longest documented boxing match of the 20th century. His career spanned the same era as Jack Johnson's.

Jack Johnson—professional record of 54 W/ 11 L 36 KO's is the first black heavyweight champion. His flamboyant personality and romantic affairs with white women are as deliberated as his boxing career.

Rocky Marciano—professional record of 49 W/ 0 L 43 KO's is known for his perfect record and Italian American iconic status.

Sam McVey—professional record of 66 W/ 13 L 52 KO's is one of the early black heavyweight boxers and is most known for his 49 round bout with Joe Jeanette: the longest boxing match of the 20th century. His career spanned the same era as Jack Johnson's.

"Sugar" Ray Robinson—professional record of 173 W/ 19 L 108 KO's is often noted as the greatest boxer of all time by sportswriters, fellow boxers, and reputable trainers. His bout with and subsequent death of Jimmy Doyle is well noted.

"Iron" Mike Tyson—professional record of 50 W/ 6 L 44 KO's was the youngest heavyweight champion of all time. His legal issues and abrupt downward spiral is the subject of much discussion.

"Cus D'Amato on Fear"—Cus D'Amato is one of the most famous boxing managers and trainers ever. In addition to discovering and training Mike Tyson, he trained Floyd Patterson and Jose Torres.

"Not Joe Frazier"—On July 26th 1986, Mike Tyson demolished the son of Joe Frazier (Marvis Frazier). Frazier was KO'd at 30 seconds in the first round, which became the fastest KO of Tyson's career.

"Jamaal X Jackson"—Viduidaes are Indigobirds indigenous to Africa.

"Undressing the Belt" refers to Tyson's bout against Frank Bruno and reclamation of the WBC title.

"Canine to Cartilage" highlights the second Mike Tyson and Evander Holyfield match in which Tyson bit off a portion of Holyfield's ear.

"Billy Boy" Billy Boy refers to Joe Frazier's childhood nickname.

"Conspiracy Theory" highlights the second Muhammad Ali and Sonny Liston match in which Ali's first round knockout of Liston- dubbed the phantom punch- has often been the subject of conspiracy theories.

"Recapping Ali Frazier I: Frank Lucas" provides voice to notorious Harlem crime boss Frank Lucas. Lucas' life was dramatized in the 2007 Universal Pictures film *American Gangster*. Denzel Washington played Frank Lucas.

"Joe Frazier and The Knockouts"—Throughout and after his boxing career, Joe Frazier sang and performed with a soul group dubbed "Joe Frazier and The Knockouts."

"Good For Nothing Joe" references a record performed by Lena Horne and written by Ted Koelher.

"Saturday Night at *Café*" references an Etta in the second stanza. The person referenced here is Etta Duryea, the first wife of Jack Johnson.

"Sam McVey"—It is documented that Jack Johnson paid for Sam McVey's headstone.

Acknowledgements

Thank you to the following journals for publishing earlier versions of these poems:

Blackbird:
"Letters to Joe Louis from Joe Frazier"

Booth:
"Jack Johnson writes Robert Delaney"
"Letters to Jack Johnson from Robert Delaney"

Brawler (online):
"The Brown Bomber Convinces Benny
He a Man"
"Constructing The New Negro"
"Marciano Deconstructs The New Negro"
"The Radio Sounds Better Than Cab Calloway
When Crooning a Louis Fight"

Callaloo:
"Jamaal Jackson converts Mike to Islam"
"Letters to Joe Frazier From Mike Tyson"
"Not Joe Frazier: Tyson Writes Apology Letter"

Pluck:
"Letters to Jack Johnson from Joe Louis"

Poetry Quarterly:
"Joe Jennette and Sam McVey Fistfight in Hell"

The Red Clay Review:
"Doormen Left and Charlie Banter Outside the Cotton Club"

Tidal Basin Review:
"Dear Darkness: Joe Frazier Writes Mike Tyson"
"Shot for Joe:
One Part Marciano / Two Parts Frazier"

Verse Wisconsin:
"Ali Frazier II: Ali's Gloves Delivers Punch line"
"Frazier Dreams in Blues"
"Mistress in Manila: Veronica Porche Testifies"
"Recapping Ali Frazier I: As Told by Ringside Journalist"

The Wisconsin Review:
"There are Ghosts Inside Here: Jack Johnson Writes Joe Louis"

I would like to thank everyone who lent a hand or eye to the poems in ROPES: Maurice Kilwein-Guevara, Rebecca Dunham, Kim Blaeser, Michael Wilson, Anika Wilson, Drew Blanchard, Randall Horton, Chiyuma Elliot, Beth Ann Fennelly, and Quraysh Ali Lansana. To my mother, Cassandra, father, Floyd, sister, Bianca, and extended family. We have so much more to do. I want to thank both the English and Afro American Studies Faculties at the University of Mississippi for welcoming and supporting me and my family with open arms. I'm grateful to work and happy hour with you all. A huge shout to the book designers: Zach Lewis and Charlie Dingus. I had a vision after a hazy dream and you brought it to life. Thank you. I will forever owe my fellow Aquarian Heather Buchanan-Gueringer for believing in my writing. I'm thankful to be a part of something special. Willow Books is something special. To my wife, April, and son, Drake, for keeping a foundation beneath my soles, thank you.

About the Poet

Derrick Harriell, Ph.D. served as Director of the African American Studies program at the University of Mississippi. He is the author of *Cotton* (2010) and *ROPES* (2013) (Willow Books), *Stripper in Wonderland* (2017) and *Come Kingdom* (2022).